RECLAIM YOUR SPACE, RECLAIM YOUR LIFE

FIND CALM, ONE STEP AT A TIME

© 2024 NEATVANA
All rights reserved. No part of this book may be reproduced, stored in a retrieval system, or transmitted in any form or by any means, electronic, mechanical, photocopying, recording, or otherwise, without the prior written permission of the publisher.

Table of Contents

Page 5: Introduction: From Chaos To Calm
Page 9: Phase 1: Reflect On Clutter Triggers
Page 17: Phase 2: Seek Help If Needed
Page 21: 3: Mindful Decluttering
Page 27: Mindful Decluttering Worksheet
Page 31: Phase 4: Sustainable System
Page 39: You've Reclaimed Your Space And Your life
Page 41: Resources And Credits
Page 44: The Neatvana Community

"Chaos doesn't own you—you've got this, one corner at a time."

Introduction

FROM CHAOS TO CALM:
The Birth of the NEATVANA-Method

Introduction:
From Chaos to Calm: Feeling stuck, ashamed and honestly, pretty lost.
Let's be honest—clutter can feel like a beast that just won't quit. I know because I've been there.
Picture this: me, standing in my living room, surrounded by piles of clothes, random papers, and dishes I swore I'd wash "tomorrow." It wasn't just a messy day—it was my life for years. I'd clean in a frenzy before guests came, only to see the mess return days later. I felt stuck, ashamed, and honestly, pretty lost.

I used to think, *"Why can't I get this under control? What's wrong with me?"* I tried all the tricks—fancy bins, decluttering apps, you name it—but nothing stuck. One tearful day, staring at the chaos, it hit me.
The clutter wasn't just stuff. It was my stress, my problems, my exhaustion, my scattered mind spilling out into my space. That's when I started digging deeper, and slowly, things changed.

First, I went to my doctor, who recommended a social worker to help me find out why I couldn't find light in that cluttered forest. I was too ashamed to talk to family or friends, but now I understand the importance of seeking support. Standing in front of my chaos, I finally said, "Enough. This is my house, and I will reclaim it." That's when I declared, "I reclaim my space, I reclaim my life!"

Introducing the Neatvana Method
It took me months—almost a year—to refine what works for me, and I'm still improving it. I wrote down everything I did, checked what worked and what didn't, and reflected on why. That's how I developed the Neatvana Method—a simple, supportive way to reclaim your space and your life by addressing both the physical and emotional sides of clutter.

Overview of the Four Phases
1. **Understand your Clutter Triggers:** We'll start by understanding what's really behind your clutter—whether it's stress, procrastination, or emotional baggage holding you back.
2. **Seek Help if Needed:** If it feels like too much to handle alone, I'll encourage you to reach out for support from friends, family, or even professionals—no shame in that!
3. **Mindful Decluttering:** Then, we'll let go of what's no longer serving you, room by room, with intention and kindness toward yourself.
4. **Sustainable Systems**: Finally, we'll set up simple, budget-friendly systems—like my Accessory Rotation System—to keep your space clear and calm for the long haul.

I'm not here to say I've got it all figured out—I'm still learning every day. But I've found ways to break that cycle, and I'd love to share them with you. That's what Reclaim Your Space, Reclaim Your Life is about. It's not me telling you what to do— it's me saying, "Hey, I've struggled with this, too. Want to work through it together?"

What This Workbook Is:
This is a space to explore why clutter keeps creeping back and how we can make our homes feel good again. I'll share my story — the messes, the realizations, the little wins — offer tools that helped me. You can try them, tweak them, or create your own. It's all about finding what works for you.

Here's what we'll do together:

- **Reflect:** Look at what's really behind the clutter (spoiler: it's not just laziness!).
- **Try Stuff Out:** Explore simple steps like rotating accessories to keep things fresh without piling up.
- **Keep It Real:** Focus on progress, not perfection.

Quick Note:
This workbook is based on my personal journey and isn't a substitute for professional therapy. If you're facing tougher challenges, please talk to a licensed professional—you deserve all the support you need.

Clutter often stems from hidden triggers—like stress, emotions, or habits—that keep it piling up. Recognizing these triggers is the key to taking control. In the following phases, we'll guide you through understanding and addressing these triggers to reclaim your space and your life.

Ready to get started?
Let's turn the page and begin with Phase 1: Reflect on Clutter Triggers.

"Mess isn't random—it's your life talking. Listen up."

Phase 1

THE NEATVANA-METHOD
Reflect on Clutter Triggers

Welcome to the First Phase of the Neatvana-Method!

As we mentioned in the introduction, clutter triggers are the root causes of why clutter accumulates. Now, let's uncover what your specific triggers might be. These triggers can vary widely, but some common ones include stressful life events, sentimental attachments to items, or simply procrastination.

Understanding what's behind your clutter is the first step to breaking free from it. To help you identify your own triggers, consider these questions:
- What situations make your clutter worse? (e.g., busy work weeks, family visits)
- When do you find yourself avoiding decluttering tasks? (e.g., when tired, overwhelmed)
- Are there certain items you struggle to let go of? (e.g., gifts, old clothes)

Use this checklist to pinpoint your personal clutter triggers:
- Stress from work or personal responsibilities
- Sentimental attachment to items
- Procrastination or feeling too tired to declutter
- Fear of needing something later
- Difficulty making decisions about what to keep
- Other: (your turn!)_____
- _____
- _____
- _____
- _____
- _____

Every small step counts—celebrate your progress!

By naming your triggers, you're already taking control. Let's move forward with this insight as we prepare to declutter mindfully.

Before we touch a single item, let's figure out why clutter keeps sneaking back into your life. This isn't just about spotting a mess—it's about understanding what's going on inside that lets it pile up. Think of it like finding the root of a weed: once you know what's feeding it, you can pull it out for good. It might feel a little overwhelming at first, but don't worry—we've all been there, and I'm right here with you.

My Story: Chaos in the Kitchen

After that tearful moment in my living room, I started asking myself why the mess kept coming back. It wasn't laziness—it was something deeper.

After that tearful moment in my living room, I started asking myself why the mess kept coming back. It wasn't laziness—it was something deeper. On stressful workdays, my kitchen turned into a war zone—no space to even set a glass down. When money or family stuff got heavy, the mail piled up on the dining table like a paper avalanche. It hit me: my space was screaming what my mind was feeling—total chaos. So I dug into why, and found out it's bigger than just stuff piling up.

I remember one particularly rough week when everything spiraled out of control. Work was hectic, I was behind on bills, and I hadn't slept well in days. My living room looked like a tornado had hit it—clothes strewn everywhere, books and magazines scattered, and a layer of dust coating every surface. I felt paralyzed, not even knowing where to begin. In that moment of frustration, it hit me:

Clutter wasn't just about the stuff. It was a symptom of how I was feeling inside. My space was reflecting my stress, my anxiety, and my exhaustion.

But here's the good news—I wasn't alone. I did I dug into why and found out that this is a journey beyond boxes. Studies show that clutter can ramp up stress, muddy our focus, and even mess with our sleep. It's not just about the mess; it's about how it weighs on us. That's why figuring out why clutter keeps coming back matters so much. Tidying up once and crossing our fingers isn't enough—we've got to dig into the root causes together.

Clutter doesn't just happen—it's often a sign of something deeper going on. Phase 1 is all about figuring out what sparks your clutter piles so you can start taking control. Let's dive in with some exercises, questions, tips, and a story to guide you along the way.

Let's get specific about your clutter triggers. Grab a notebook and set aside a few minutes for this prompt:

"Write about a time when your clutter felt completely out of control. What was happening in your life then? What specific items piled up, and why do you think that was?"

Maybe it was during a hectic week when mail and takeout containers swallowed your kitchen counter. Or perhaps a tough life moment left you surrounded by clothes you couldn't bring yourself to sort. Don't overthink it—just write what comes to mind. This isn't about judgment; it's about spotting patterns. Seeing the "why" behind your clutter is the first step to tackling it.

_____
_____
_____
_____
_____
_____
_____
_____
_____
_____
_____
_____
_____
_____
_____
_____
_____
_____
_____
_____
_____
_____
_____

Now, let's broaden the picture. These questions will help you connect your clutter triggers to your everyday life and feelings. You can write your answers or just mull them over:

How do your clutter triggers affect your daily life?
- Does a messy desk zap your focus? Does a cluttered living room make it hard to unwind? *Seeing the damage shows why it's worth fixing.*

_____
_____
_____
_____
_____
_____
_____

- What emotions come up when you think about letting go of certain items? Are you hit with guilt, nostalgia, or maybe a flicker of excitement?

_____
_____
_____
_____
_____
_____
_____

Are there specific rooms or areas where clutter always seems to creep back? What's going on there? Is it a procrastination hotspot or a stress dumping ground? Knowing your clutter's favorite hangouts is key to breaking the cycle.
Take your time with these—they're like a flashlight illuminating your clutter story.

_____
_____
_____
_____
_____
_____
_____

Practical Tips for Common Triggers

Clutter triggers vary, but some solutions fit like a glove no matter who you are. Here are a few to try, tailored to common culprits:

- **Stress:** When life's a whirlwind, clutter can feel paralyzing. Set a 10-minute timer and clear one small spot—like a nightstand or a corner of the couch. It's quick, it's doable, and it's a little boost when you need it most.
- **Sentimental Attachment:** Letting go of treasures can sting. Try taking a photo of the item to keep the memory alive. That way, you can pass it on without feeling like you're losing the past.
- **Procrastination:** If "later" is your go-to, test the "one-touch trick." Pick up an item and decide its fate right then—keep it, donate it, or toss it. It's a tiny shift that keeps piles from growing.

These are starting points—tweak them to match your vibe. You're the boss of your clutter journey.

Common Clutter Triggers
So, why does clutter keep sneaking back into our lives? Here are a few culprits I've spotted in my own journey—see if any sound familiar to you:
- **Stress:** When work deadlines loom, money problems and life gets wild, tidying up slides to the bottom of the list. It's tough to muster the energy to clean when you're running on empty.
- **Life Transitions:** Big shifts—like moving, starting a new job, or navigating a breakup—can throw your routines off-kilter, letting clutter creep in.
- **Emotional Overwhelm:** Sometimes we cling to things for sentimental reasons or dodge decisions about what to keep because it feels too heavy.

These triggers can catch us off guard, turning a neat space into chaos before we know it. But spotting them is the first step to breaking free.

Your Clutter Trigger Summary:
Jot down your top triggers based on your reflections
[ ] _____
[ ] _____
[ ] _____
[ ] _____
[ ] _____
[ ] _____
[ ] _____
[ ] _____
[ ] _____
[ ] _____
[ ] _____
[ ] _____
[ ] _____
[ ] _____
[ ] _____

Naming your triggers is a big deal—it's the first step to understanding your clutter story.

"Stuck? Tell someone—it's not weak, it's smart."

Phase 2

THE NEATVANA-METHOD
Seek Help if Needed

Welcome to Phase 2!

You've just taken a big step by reflecting on your clutter triggers—way to go! Now, let's talk about something quick but powerful: it's okay to ask for help when you feel stuck. Clutter isn't just about stuff—it can glue you to the floor with emotions, stress, and problems you didn't even know were there. I've been in that spot, and I want you to know there's no shame in reaching out. This step is all about finding the support you need to move forward, in your own way.

Why Help Can Change Everything
When clutter piles up, it's often a sign of bigger things going on—like stress or chaos you can't quite pin down. For me, I thought I had to fix it all alone, but I learned that asking for help can shine a light on what's really holding you back. This step is short because I'm not here to tell you exactly who to call—I'm not a pro, and you're the one who knows what feels right. It could be a friend, family, a doctor, a therapist—whatever helps you unstick yourself.

My Story: Uncovering the Real Mess
When my kitchen turned into a disaster zone—dishes everywhere, papers piling up—I was too embarrassed to tell family or friends. I felt like they'd judge me for letting it get so bad. So, I went to my doctor instead, and he sent me to a social worker. She didn't touch my clutter—she helped me figure out why it was taking over my home and my life. Turns out, my messy space was tied to bigger issues I didn't even see: work stress draining me, family and friends wearing me out without me noticing, and a pile of administration I couldn't face. She pointed me to help with paperwork, set boundaries with people who were wearing me out, and even sent me to therapy for deeper stuff I hadn't realized was there. As I started sorting out those pieces, I could finally breathe—and that's when I began tackling the clutter at home on my own terms.

How to Know You Need Help
If your clutter feels like a heavy weight—if emotions, stress, or problems make you feel stuck to the spot—it's time to reach out. You don't need all the answers; just take one step toward support. Here are some ideas:

- **A Friend:** Someone to talk it out or keep you company while you sort.
- **Family:** A loved one to lift you up when you're down.
- **A Pro**: A doctor, therapist, or social worker if it's more than just stuff—like it was for me.
- **Church:** you can find help in your church

Quick Tip:
Try saying, "I'm feeling stuck—can you help me figure this out?" It's simpler than you think.

Your Turn:
Who's Your Lifeline?
Grab a pen and write down one person (or resource) you could turn to if you feel stuck. It might be a friend's name, a family member, or a helpline—whatever feels safe.

Who's got my back: _____

Why them? Maybe they're a great listener or just get you—pick what works for you.
_____
_____
_____
_____

Why This Step Rocks
This isn't about fixing your clutter right away—it's about finding help for the stuff behind it, like I did. When I reached out, I didn't just clear my space; I got to know myself better and spotted my triggers. You're the one who knows what you need, and that's your strength.

Ready for **Phase 3: Mindful Decluttering**?

With your triggers in sight and a lifeline ready, you're set to start decluttering with intention.

"One drawer, 15 minutes—chaos doesn't stand a chance."

Phase 3

THE NEATVANA-METHOD
Mindful Decluttering

Welcome to Phase 3!

You've reflected on your clutter triggers and thought about who's got your back—awesome work! Now, it's time to start decluttering with intention, one small step at a time. This isn't about rushing to perfection or clearing everything in one go—it's about letting go of what no longer serves you, with kindness and care. I've been where you are, and I'll share how I figured this out so we can do it together.

Why Mindful Decluttering Works
Clutter can feel like a mountain, but breaking it into bite-sized pieces makes it doable. This step is all about sorting your space with purpose—not just tossing stuff, but asking yourself what fits the life you want right now. It's gentle, it's yours, and it's how I turned my chaos into calm.

"Clutter's just life yelling—quiet it down, bit by bit."

My Story: From Chaos to Calm
When I decided to tackle my kitchen, I was brimming with determination. I thought, "Three hours, and it'll be clutter-free!" So, I dove in, pulling everything out of the drawers—spoons, lids, gadgets—and spreading it all across the counters and dining table. An hour and a half later, though, I was staring at a mess bigger than when I started. I felt overwhelmed and mad at myself. I'd bitten off way more than I could chew, and I was stuck. Defeated, I made a cup of tea, sat down, and didn't get up again. For the next few days, I couldn't even cook—every surface was buried under chaos, and all I could focus on was what I hadn't done.

After a few days of avoiding the disaster zone, I knew I couldn't keep living like that. I had to try something different. I grabbed my tablet, set a timer for 30 minutes, and told myself, "Just sort what you want to keep." I picked up each item and asked, *"Why do I want this?"* The things I wanted went back in the drawers. When the timer buzzed, I stopped, took a walk to clear my head, and came back feeling lighter. I ate some fruit, reset the timer for another 30 minutes, and tackled the broken stuff—cracked containers and rusty utensils went straight to the trash. In a third 30-minute session, I boxed up extras for the second-hand store. By the end of those three hours, my kitchen was usable again, and the drawers had way less junk.

Two days later, I refined my approach. I switched to 15-minute bursts and focused on one drawer at a time. I'd clean it out, add dividers or lid holders. When the timer went off, I'd open and close the drawer a few times, grinning at how neat it looked—proud I'd made it work, and check my work: *"Can I see everything? Can I grab it easily? Can I put it back just as easily?"*. I kept that rhythm going: 15 to 30 minutes of decluttering, then a break to walk, sip tea, or just relax.

Over the next two weeks, I worked through six big drawers, a freezer, a fridge, a coffee machine, two tall cabinets, a combi-microwave, an air fryer, and six small cabinets. Each session was short, but they added up.

Along the way, I figured out something big:
When I pushed past 30 minutes, I'd get drained, and the clutter would somehow look worse. But sticking to short bursts—15 or 30 minutes—kept me energized and in control. I wasn't tired or discouraged anymore; I was excited. Every time I finished a drawer or cabinet, I'd feel a little burst of pride. Two weeks might sound slow, but those small wins stacked up, and celebrating them kept me motivated.

I also took before and after pictures, which turned out to be a game-changer. Seeing the progress visually gave me a boost to keep going. After finishing a drawer or cabinet, I'd test it out—open it, close it, grab something, put it back—just to make sure it worked for me. And celebrate that I did it!

And once I'd decluttered something, I made a point to keep it clean when I used it.

How to Declutter Mindfully
Here's how you can start:

- **Pick One Room:** (example the kitchen) break it down in small pieces. Write down on the worksheet how many drawers, cabinets the kitchen has, refrigerator freezer, microwave etc etc.
- **Make a before picture**
- **Set a Timer:** Try 15 or 30 minutes—whatever feels good. Little bursts beat giant messes.
- **Sort with Intention:** Use these three categories:
1. Keep: Items you use often or that spark joy.
2. Donate: Things in good shape someone else could use.
3. Discard: Anything broken, expired, or past its prime.
- **Take Breaks:** When the timer's up, step away—stretch, sip something, recharge.
- **Celebrate Every Bit:** Even one cleared shelf is a win—give yourself a cheer!
- M**ake an after picture**

Quick Tip:
If it feels tough, go back to your triggers from Step 1—they'll guide you on what to let go.

Hey there! I'm excited to walk you through how the blocks, circles, and stars work together—it's a super simple system to help you tackle decluttering step by step. Think of it like a friendly little guide to keep you on track. Let's break it down!

Your Decluttering Map
Imagine a rectangle divided into smaller blocks—like a grid or a map. Each block stands for one small area in your space that you want to declutter, like a drawer, a shelf, or even that tricky corner of your room. This is your decluttering map, and it's here to make the whole process feel less overwhelming by splitting it into bite-sized pieces.

How the Blocks Work
Here's the fun part: each block is like its own mini-project.

To get started:
Label the Blocks: Write the name of each area you want to declutter inside its own block. For example, if you're working on your bedroom, you might write "closet" in one block, "nightstand" in another, and "under the bed" in a third. Now you've got a clear picture of your room, broken down into manageable chunks.

Pick One: Choose a block to start with—any one you like! Don't do them all at once; just focus on one area at a time.

Circles and Stars: Your Progress Trackers
Inside each block, you'll see two little symbols: a circle and a star.

Here's how they work with the blocks to keep you moving forward:
- ○ **Circle:**

When you begin decluttering the area in that block, color in the circle. It's like giving yourself a little high-five—"Hey, I've started this!"
- ☆ **Star:**

Once you've finished decluttering that area, color in the star. This is your moment to shine—"Woohoo, I did it!" It's a tiny celebration for completing that mini-project.

So, as you go through each block, the circle and star help you track your progress: the circle marks the start, and the star marks the finish. Easy, right?

A Quick Example
Let's say your bedroom has a few blocks: "closet," "bed," "nightstand," etc.

- You decide to start with the closet. When you begin sorting through it, you color in the circle in the "closet" block.
- Once you've finished decluttering the closet—everything's organized and looking great—you color in the star. Done!
- Then, you move on to the next block you want, coloring its circle when you start and its star when you finish. One block at a time, you're making progress!

Bonus: Add a Little Color (Optional)
If you're feeling extra reflective, you can color the star based on how the decluttering felt:
Color examples: Pick any color that vibes with you!.
Green: If that area was easy to start and finish.
Yellow: If it was a bit tough to get going or wrap up.

This part's totally up to you—no pressure! It's just a fun way to look back and see what worked for you.

Why It's Awesome
The blocks give you a clear plan, and the circles and stars make it exciting to see how far you've come. It's like turning decluttering into a little game—start with a circle, finish with a star, and watch your space transform, one block at a time. You've got this!

"Jot it, sort it, own it—one space at a time."

ROOM DECLUTTERING
WORKSHEET

SPACE DETAILS
Room/Area I'm Decluttering: _____
How do you feel   : _____
_____

Acknowledge how you feel, be honest.
Remember it's not a competition, it's about you!

STEP 1: CHOOSE YOUR FOCUS AREA
- Make a picture
- Specify the blocks in the areas of the room
- Get your cleaning products ready
- Boxes and bags for the sorting
- Set the timer 15 - 30 minutes

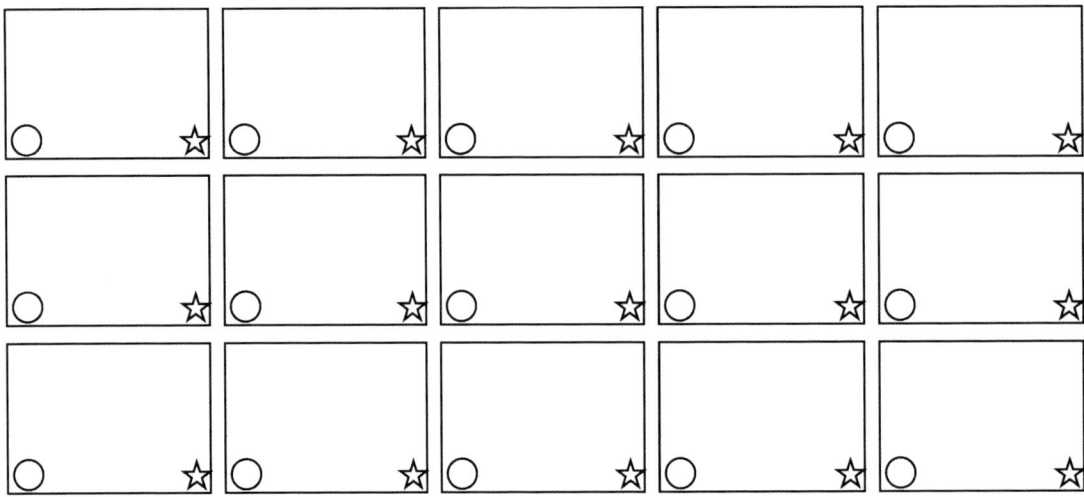

STEP 2:
THOUGHTFUL SORTING
Grab stuff easy from your chosen area and consider each one as you sort into:

[ ] **KEEP:** Use regularly, works well, brings joy
[ ] **DONATE:** Good items you don't use (*must deliver within 3 days or discard*)
[ ] **DISCARD:** Expired, broken, or duplicates
[ ] **RELOCATE:** Belongs elsewhere

Questions to ask yourself:
-When did I last use this? Would I buy this again today? Do I have multiples of this item?
Does this deserve the space it takes?-

STEP 3:
CLEAN THE EMPTY SPACE
[ ] **Wipe down** all surfaces of the area
[ ] **Check** for needed repairs
[ ] **Measure** available space: _____ × _____ × _____

This serves two key purposes:
  1. Helps you be more mindful about what will actually fit when you return items
  2. Gives you measurements if you want to buy organizers or containers

STEP 4: ORGANIZE & RETURN ITEMS

Now it's time to put everything back in a way that makes sense for you. Sort your items however feels natural—maybe by how often you use them, by category, by size, or something else entirely. Play around until it clicks for your space. No need to write it all down—just dive in and organize!

Optional: If you want, jot down a quick note below about what worked well or anything you might tweak next time.

_____
_____
_____
_____
_____
_____
_____
_____
_____
_____
_____
_____
_____

Take a moment to test your new setup!
Open and close drawers and doors a few times.
For shelves, practice taking items out and putting them back in place.
This quick check ensures your organization actually works for you and gives you a joyful, proud or any positive feeling.

STEP 5: CELEBRATE YOUR PROGRESS

You've made it—awesome job! Grab your phone and snap an "after" photo of your space to see the difference it makes. Then, take a sec to write down how you feel now compared to before. Does it feel calmer? Lighter? Whatever's on your mind, jot it down.

How I Feel Now:
What's different? How does this space feel to you now?
_____
_____
_____
_____

Tip:
If you've got a "before" photo, take a peek at it now—check out how far you've come!

Phase 4

THE NEATVANA-METHOD
Sustainable Systems

Phase 4: Sustainable Systems for a Clutter-Free Life

Welcome to Phase 4!

You've done the hard work of reflecting on your clutter triggers, seeking support, and mindfully decluttering your space—great job! You've cleared the clutter and reclaimed your space—amazing work! Now, Phase 4 is all about keeping that calm, clutter-free vibe going strong. This isn't about starting over every week—it's about setting up simple, sustainable habits that fit your life and keep your home peaceful without stress.

In this phase, I'll share a few of my favorite tricks on simple to get you started. We'll cover:
1. **Cleaning calendar** - Creating your own Cleaning Calendar
2. **Family Teamwork** - Tips for Families and Kids
3. **The Birthday Hack** - hack that never gets old
4. **Bedding Basics** - Keep them fresh and neat

Let's break this down. Ready? Let's roll!

1. **Cleaning calendar** - Creating your own Cleaning Calendar

I could give you a one-size-fits-all calendar, but here's the truth: your home, your family, and your rhythms are unique. What works for me might not work for you—and that's okay! By now, you've got the tools from Phases 1-3 to figure out what keeps your space calm and clutter-free.

Let's make it personal: Create Your Own Cleaning Calendar
Grab a pen and a blank sheet (or use your phone)—it's time to design a decluttering plan that fits you. Think about your home's hotspots—those places clutter loves to sneak back into—like the kitchen counter, kids' rooms, or your desk.
Then, decide what small tasks you can do daily, weekly, monthly, or even yearly to stay on top of it.

Here's a little nudge to get you started:
- **Daily:** Kitchen counter, dishwasher, toys, etc.
- **Weekly:** Tidy a drawer / shelf, bedding, toilet, refrigerator, etc.
- **Monthly:** Swap out seasonal, freezer, doors (frames) etc
- **Yearly:** Deep-cleaning: carpet, behind large appliances, etc.

Set a timer for the tasks—it keeps them quick and easy! Not sure where to begin? Check online for tons of calendar ideas—there are so many examples out there to inspire you. Pick what clicks, tweak it, and make it your own.

Why This Works for You
You're in charge now. You know your triggers, you've decluttered with intention, and you've got the power to decide how to maintain it. This isn't about me telling you what to do—it's about you building a system that feels good and sticks.

Craving more tricks to play with? My next book will dive deeper into sustainable systems for every corner of your home—stay tuned!

2. **Family Teamwork:** Tips for Families and Kids

Decluttering with a family can feel overwhelming—especially with kids who collect toys, clothes, and random "treasures" faster than you can blink. But here's the upside: getting the kids involved not only keeps your home tidy but also teaches them responsibility and organization skills they'll carry into life. Plus, it turns decluttering into a team effort that lifts everyone up.

A Cluttered Home Affects the Whole Family
A cluttered home doesn't just stress you and your partner out—it throws the whole crew off balance. Kids might struggle to focus, relax, or even find their favorite stuffed animal in the chaos. But it's more than that: growing up in clutter can mean they miss out on learning how to keep their own space clean and organized.
Kids do what they see—if they watch you and your partner prioritize a tidy home and pitch in, they'll start to value it too.

On the flip side, if parents always do it all, kids might grow up expecting someone else to handle everything—now and even later in life.

Studies show this can lead to less independence and confidence down the road, leaving teens or adults kinda loss to manage their own spaces or responsibilities because they never got the chance to learn.

By setting up systems where the whole family—kids and partners included—works together, you're not just creating a calmer, happier home for now; you're giving your kids habits that'll help them thrive in the future. It's a win-win for everyone!

Teamwork Lightens the Load: When the family tackles it together, you're not stuck doing it no "All by Myself"(Celine Dion moments here, ha ha!). It's quicker, easier, and honestly, way more fun.

How to Get Everyone Involved
Let's make decluttering a family affair—here are some practical ways to rope in the kids, no matter their age:

- **Morning Bed-Making Ritual:** Kick off the day together by making beds. For little ones, you or your partner might do most of it, but let them fluff a pillow or tuck in a stuffed animal. Older kids can handle their own bed—ask if they need help or can manage solo, giving them the choice between independence or teamwork. Both are great! Partners can join in by making their side or helping the kids—it's a quick family win.
- **Nightly Tidy-Up Time:** Set a timer for 5-10 minutes before bed and have everyone pitch in—kids putting away toys, straightening desks, or grabbing stray shoes, while partners tackle their own spots like the coffee table or kitchen counter. Turn it into a game with a fun reward, like a quick dance party or an extra bedtime story.
- **Age-Appropriate Tasks:** Match the jobs to their stage:
  - **Toddlers:** Hand them a toy to toss in a bin while you or your partner cheer them on.
  - **School-Age Kids**: Let them sort their books or clothes (with a little nudging if needed).
  - **Teens:** Give them ownership of their room or a shared space like the living room.
  - **Partner:** They can take on a shared area—like clearing the entryway or organizing the garage—to keep the load balanced.
- **Lead by Example:** Show them how you tidy your own stuff—your desk, closet, whatever. Talk it out: "I'm putting this here so I can find it later." It's less about telling them what to do and more about letting them see it in action from both of you.

Tips to Keep It Fun
- *Timer Challenges: Kids love a race—set a 10-minute timer and see how much you can all get done.*
- *Celebrate the Wins: Reward the effort with a snack, a family movie, or just a big "We rocked this!" hug.*
- *Go Easy: It doesn't have to be perfect—focus on them trying, not the end result.*
- *Make It a Team Thing: Point out how a tidy home means more room for fun stuff—playing, relaxing, or just hanging out together.*

3. **The Birthday Hack** - Hack that never gets old

Birthdays can pile up stress and stuff—presents, cards, and last-minute chaos. Here's my hack to keep it simple and clutter-free: plan ahead! You already know when your loved ones' birthdays are, so use that to your advantage.

How It Works
- **For Kids:** Buy gifts during sales or outlet periods—think post-holiday deals or summer clearances. Hide 'em smart (a labeled box works great) until the big day. No rush, no extra clutter!
- **For Cards:** Make your own or snag them cheap during sales. Keep a small stash ready to go.
- **For You:** When people ask what you want, say "gift cards!" I've trained my crew to stick to this—it cuts down on random stuff I don't need, and I can pick what I love later.

Why It's a Win
This keeps your home free of gift clutter and your wallet happy. It's a sustainable system that saves time, money, and space—plus, you're always ready to celebrate without the scramble!

4. **Bedding Basics** - Keep them fresh and neat

Your bedroom should be a peaceful spot, not a clutter trap full of extra sheets and blankets.

Here's a trick I swear by:
stick to just two sets of bedding per bed—one on the bed, one washed and ready to go. When it's laundry day, swap them out: wash the used set, dry it, fold it, and store it neatly until next time. That's it—no piles of extras, no mess!

Why It Works
Two sets do the trick: one to use, one as a backup. It cuts down on clutter in your closet or drawers, saves you from drowning in laundry, and keeps your bedroom feeling fresh and simple. No more wondering where all those spare sheets came from or why they're taking up space! Plus, it's a small habit that makes a big difference— less stuff means less stress.

How to Make It Happen
- Pick your two favorite sets per bed—ones you love to sleep in.
- Donate or repurpose any extras (old sheets make great rags or picnic blankets!).
- Find a spot for the spare set—like a shelf or bin—so it's easy to grab when you need it.
- Swap and wash weekly or whenever works for you—just keep it consistent.

Tip:
Try one set in a calm, solid color (like a soft blue or white) for a soothing vibe, and one cheerful set with flowers or a design you adore to switch things up when you're feeling fancy!

This little system keeps your bedroom neat and your mind calm—sustainable living, one bed at a time!

"Set it up once, keep it calm forever—your way."

Conclusion

THE NEATVANA-METHOD
You've Reclamed Your Space and Your Live

Wow, Look at You!

Take a deep breath and give yourself a huge round of applause—you've made it through the Neatvana Method! From reflecting on what was holding you back, to finding support when you needed it, clearing out the clutter with care, and setting up simple systems to keep it that way, you've done something incredible. You didn't just tidy up a room; you reclaimed your space and, with it, a piece of your peace, your energy, and your joy.

This journey wasn't always easy—trust me, I know! There were probably moments of doubt, maybe a few tears, and definitely some "why did I keep this?" surprises along the way. But every step you took brought you here: a home that feels lighter, calmer, and more you. And the best part? You've built skills and habits that'll stick with you—not just for now, but for life.

What You've Gained
- **A clearer space** that reflects who you are and how you want to live.
- **The confidence** to let go of what doesn't serve you—stuff, stress, or even old habits.
- **A family team** (if you've got one) that's in it together, learning and growing with you.
- **Simple systems**—like your birthday trick or bedding setup—that make calm the new normal.

The Road Ahead: *This isn't the end—it's a beginning!*
You've got the tools to keep your space clutter-free, and every little win builds on the last. Want more ideas to make it even easier? My next book's coming with deeper hacks and systems to keep your whole home humming along. For now, enjoy this moment.

Now, take a moment to look around your space and celebrate how far you've come. You've reclaimed your space—and your life. What's your next small step?.

One Last Thing
Decluttering isn't about perfection—it's about progress. You've started something powerful here, and it's yours to keep growing. So, here's to you, your space, and the life you're reclaiming—one neat, happy corner at a time. You've got this!

THE NEATVANA-METHOD
Recourses and Credits

Books:
- The Life-Changing Magic of Tidying Up by Marie Kondo
- Atomic Habits by James Clear.

Studies:
- Research on the psychological effects of clutter, including increased stress and reduced focus, is supported by studies such as Saxbe and Repetti's work published in the *Personality and Social Psychology Bulletin* (2010).
- Research on the impact of cluttered environments on children's development, including reduced independence and confidence, is supported by findings from Dr. Sheryl Burgstahler at the University of Washington.

"What's one thing you'd love to find under all that clutter?"

THE NEATVANA-METHOD
Neatvana Community

JOIN THE NEATVANA COMMUNITY

Thank you for reading "Reclaim Your Space, Reclaim Your Life." Your decluttering journey doesn't end here—it's just beginning!

Connect with me and fellow declutterers for ongoing support, inspiration, and tips:

Instagram: @neatvana
Facebook: Neatvana Brand
Pinterest: @neatbrand0677
TikTok: @neatvana

ENHANCE YOUR DECLUTTERING WITH MUSIC

Experience the power of music to motivate your cleaning and organization:

Listen to "The Neatvana Method" album on all streaming platforms: here are 3

youtube music   amazon music   spotify

SHARE YOUR TRANSFORMATION

I'd love to see your decluttering success! Tag your before/after photos with #NeatvanaMethod for a chance to be featured on our social media.

Visit www.neatvana.com for additional resources, worksheets, and support on your journey to a calmer, more organized life.

Made in the USA
Coppell, TX
17 June 2025